IRISH ARTS CENTER Book Day 2023

FRIDAY, MARCH 17

IN ASSOCIATION WITH
New York City Council, New York State Assembly,
New York State Senate, Lambda Literary
and Literature Ireland

WITH GENEROUS SUPPORT FROM
The Society of the Friendly Sons of St. Patrick of New York
and the Adrian Brinkerhoff Poetry Foundation

IRISHARTSCENTER.ORG | #IACBOOKDAY

Gallery Books
Editor Peter Fallon
STRAWBERRY THIEF

Sara Berkeley

STRAWBERRY THIEF

Gallery Books

Strawberry Thief
is first published
simultaneously in paperback
and in a clothbound edition
on 31 August 2005.

The Gallery Press
Loughcrew
Oldcastle
County Meath
Ireland

*All rights reserved. For permission
to reprint or broadcast these poems,
write to The Gallery Press.*

© Sara Berkeley 2005

ISBN 1 85235 388 0 *paperback*
     1 85235 389 9 *clothbound*

A CIP catalogue record for this book
is available from the British Library.

Contents

PART ONE
Feet First
   The Call *page* 13
   Smoke from Oregon Fires 14
   Strawberry Thief 15
   Freshwater Pearls 16
   Feet First 17
   Star 18
   Dogwood and Iris 20

PART TWO
The Burning Building
   My First Day in the Burning Building 23
   Wedding Day 25
   Cowboy Café, Sixty-four Miles Ahead 26
   Great Basin, April 1997 27
   First Faun 28
   Before the Wind 30
   Searchlight 31
   Patagonia 32
   Dillon Beach 33
   Last Winter 34
   The Signing 35
   Harmless 36
   Dragonflies 37
   Seven White Deer 38
   Alstroemeria 40
   The River Daughter 41
   Limpets 42
   Hawkesbury River, NSW 43
   Big Island Dance 44
   Approaching Thirty 46

PART THREE
234a Railroad
    Emergence 49
    Venus Awake 50
    Musketeer 51
    234a Railroad 52
    Architrave 53
    How We Meet 54
    What I Move To 56
    Being in the Cave before Time 57
    Eight Months, Fifteen Days 58
    A Thousand Letters 60
    Nereid 61
    Still Life, Yellow Quilt 62

Acknowledgements

Acknowledgements are made to the editors and publishers of the following where some of these poems have previously appeared: *At the Year's Turning* (Dedalus), *The Backyards of Heaven* (Scop), *Birmingham Poetry Review*, *The Black Mountain Review*, *The Burning Bush*, *The Canyon Echo*, *De Brakke Hond* (Peter Pauwels), *The Great American Poetry Show*, *Human Rights Have No Borders* (Marino), *Icarus*, *The Irish Times*, *Lectio*, *Marin Poetry Anthology* (Marin Poetry Center), *Octavo*, *On the Page*, *Poetry Ireland Review*, *Web del Sol* and *The White Page* (Salmon).

for Jessica Charlotte

PART ONE

Feet First

The Call

The Fall winds covered my bed with a sheet of leaves;
drought in much of the country, fires already.
I was dry in my skeleton, old bones
crackling in their sleep beneath the duck down,
dreams like teasing sheep's wool through a dark hole.

I thought I was a member of ordinary time,
two Sundays after the Ascension, or was it the Assumption?
But then she was here, new under the sun;
she examined every leaf, one by one by one;
she rolled on the bed laughing, and I joined in.

Hail to her, and sunlight, and spirit songs.
She bends the back of the wind and lets it go
so it springs forward with a shower of bright stars.
I touch her tiny shoulder blades as a gentle reminder —
she'll be my flown one; I will call after her

and my call will go higher and higher
till it's just air and only dolphins hear it.

Smoke from Oregon Fires

I have driven us out to the farthest parking lot,
close to the cliffs, where my hunger for flight is appeased.
Fall, obediently grey with light rain, hugs the car.
I drift around the shallows of my daughter's sleep;
I would row through it, but she never goes that deep.

When I sit with her in the dark, my arms around
the generous mercies, her childhood memories
are patchworked in the velvet corners of the room,
and round the frog walls streams
the endless ribbon of her nursery rhyme dreams.

She knew she was a girl, knew she would be born
feet first into this silvery world without consent
to decades of continuous sun and decades of snow,
but she couldn't have known her beauty
would be held up to the light and the light would drown in it.

I have her by heart, I recite her, and then she changes
and I'm lost, as if in space, end over end.
Up north of us the firemen are losing ground
to fire; their smoke comes down this far
and smudges out the still October air,

and in our car I'm listening,
and I'm noticing her hair,
the way it's still so fine and fair,
and I am listening to her breathe, and I am
listening to her breathe,
and I am listening to her breathe.

Strawberry Thief

You were a lot like planting a garden.
The seed, for example, buried deep in September,
the smell of raw lumber as we made the beds,
sun on my belly as though the sun could grow you,
and me on my knees in the heavy Spring,
labouring.

Bean seedling, starting with that soft, divided green,
already you are wild thyme, climbing rose, strawberry thief.
I cannot contain you, you send out shoots
beneath the wooden beds, coming up all daisy-eyed
among the raspberry canes, arms full of Douglas cones,
singing in your tiny cage of bird bones.

The last October sun is at our door,
the purple stars still cluster by the stairs;
any day the rain will come for our parade,
but I am gardening now, I am alone and on my knees,
the earth is warm and, if I can help you bloom,
you will be pollen for the bees;

you will shimmer in the lily beds,
shake out your petals in the breeze;
you will wear your fuchsia tutu and plié where you please
and you will leave me where I am
among the secrets of your growing.
My runner bean, with all the passion of your running
and the greenness of your going,
you lay me bare, you are my undoing.

Freshwater Pearls

I know all the days since you arrived.
I can count them like the friendly stars
or string them on a thread like freshwater pearls
and wear them about my body.

Spring is coming close enough to touch: the froth
on apple boughs, the half-winds, the scanty oaks.
I am writing it all down for you, I am painting it,
trying to find a lid to fit the box.
How much will be enough?

Look at the company you keep:
a morning glory that you picked for me,
a crushed leaf,
some tiny stones for me to shy into the creek.

Down at the beach
we sit in the lee of a dune and watch the peeled world,
naked and honest and raw to each wave,
and, every time, the writing's getting washed away.

I cup my fist around the trickling sand,
watch you chase another impossible bird,
and slowly I can start to see:
this is how today is made,
a luscious stretch of over-abundant blue,
the naked body of a tree washed smooth,
and you in your water shoes, without a limit on your love.

You are coming down the present in your short dress;
you have not done this before, alive in your first April,
but this is your stride, the rhythm of arrival,
and you carry the moment aloft,
brimming, like water in a silver cup.

Feet First

We stand in each other's light
where there is no shadow.
In the luxury of our garden
it's night, the stars are out,
the lilies balance carefully in the dark;
we take what's offered.

When we were barely begun
we cut our white hearts out
and hung them above the hungry crowd.
Towards the second month I lost the fear
that we would trip and fall,
that love would spill.

Then our traveller
swam so near us in the blind waters,
raised her hand to us, all five fingers,
brushed me with her lashes,
headstrong under the forbidden rib;
this was our promise.

When she was born
deep in the innocence of early June
the days ached to be longer
and the dawns fired up blue in our veins.
We took down our bleached hearts
and wrapped them around her.

Out of the waters where we drowned
we're laughing and the tears are coming down.
We hold her up, my bellyful of secrets,
and her breathing is enough,
her bracelet wrists,
her first foot.

Star

The Pink Ladies line our street
nodding in the loose September sun,
the money is all gone, but let me dream
now that there is, at last, time.

I dream of my daughter's wild, enthusiastic run,
our chase in this afternoon's wind
across the grassy hills, and of her grin,
all pearly bottom teeth,
and the butterfly dress she was in.

A small animal
birthed in a hidden place,
she has run me to the end of running.
I hold my side: the pain of love like mine
comes on when I'm alone.

Real summer is over, this is Indian now,
crickets own the nights.
I stand at the back door listening to the dark
feral heart of the yard with its mothy air
beating dusty and winged.
Night-lizards scramble in the dead leaves there

and in our bed
my lover's arms are open wide —
come ride it out with me,
the pain of love like ours,

and let us put out all the lights,
for in her tiny room our daughter
reaches into the future with a fearless burn,
time in spirals down her slender arms.

We do not need the stars
she will consume on her return;
we have our own.

Dogwood and Iris

Above the valley fog, below the snow,
we're looking for gold,
and here's the sun, proving
by the cut of shadows and the play of leaves
that there is more to now than what we see.

In fact, since April is the time for iris,
purple-frilled and curiously low to the ground,
we have struck it rich; the old
dogwood by the covered bridge
shines out among the river's things,
and there it is: the gold of poppies in the weeds.

On our return
the fire glows, the milk is warm,
the radio announces sunset at 7:24.
You want to see those poppies in a jar,
but I tell you in late afternoon
they fold up tight against the coming dark.

The irises have hunkered down.
I watch the sun lose power
and hold for comfort to the thought
that every day is borrowed time, and to the memory
of the dogwood blossom nobody can see,
and the gold we didn't mine.

PART TWO
The Burning Building

My First Day in the Burning Building

Marrakesh, April 1995

Out through the Dades Valley gates,
so hopelessly ornate, announcing everything,
and on to the desert, always a woman.
Mother, I look so harsh in her light,
caught between two halves
of milky amethyst, womb and brain,
and bathed in the thoughts that dry there.

We follow the line of telegraph poles
across the shale to Merzouga,
where the dunes have crouched for a thousand years.
The café owner says
his family were nomads; then they built houses.
He has never travelled far. He tells us
all the colours that the dunes can be.
I sit on the sand, looking at sand,
and watch myself burning.

Last night on Rue Mohammed Cinq
a man haggled for silver. Five days his wife,
and shaped already to the twisted shell,
I burrowed further; then,
my soft body crammed into that narrow place,
I set my pearls alight.

I wake to the tick of the dry air,
yellow huntress sun, risen without anger.
I know the day I drove those country roads,
my china flowers in my china lap,
I could have traced his contours with my eyes closed.
But that was the surface, just the beginning,

my first day in the burning building
and, under my white dress,
the silks groaned like ice.

Wedding Day

On our wedding day
under the canopy
each in our element
as though love were not
the bitterest fruit.

Cowboy Café, Sixty-four Miles Ahead

You drove faster as I fell,
stirred my rapid dreams.
I woke as we sped towards a wooden bridge.
It seemed to span
the world of sound and the world of space;
you spun us around, you laughed and said
we were winning the human race.

Pahrump, Nopah, the big Death Valley in white stones
set in the hillside just beyond Shoshone —
'NEXT SERVICES 51 MILES' —
across the Amargosa, through the Owlshead hills.

We took 178
through Salsberry Pass at three thousand feet;
snow made the rocks
fill out the shapes the Navajo had named.

The earth grew tiny, blue-green
in our rear-view mirror;
winter blew out her cold smoke in a thin stream:
I no longer believed you knew where we were going.

Cold as a queen on her king-size bed,
I had to see further.
So at Dante's View you gave me the devil's telescope:
nothing between me and the six thousand stars,
Nova Cygni, a violent brother among the girls,
and ahead, the primitive road, the Badwater,
all browns and greys, and Februaries.

Great Basin, April 1997

Quite by chance
I am set down
in the desert spring.
I hold the sand to me,
I bunch my hand around the hour,
but it's always running out.

A bird hops by with a short leg,
one foot gone — I hate the animal savagery
of pain, that hamstrung donkey
up at Kumiva Point.
I cried in the tent last night,
one of those slow dawns,
nursing my own hurt limbs,
my body learning another lesson.

And I'm still blind,
sensing the evening primrose,
velvet white, near today's campsite,
brittlebrush by feel, birdcage,
skeletonweed blowing by,
juniper by scent, and mormon tea,
and pine. Maybe death
is no desire for any other time.

Where is the truth of all my situations?
The daylight flickers,
and I, too easily obscured,
hunker down near the rim of the world,
no idea what day it is, what colour.

First Faun

Late Winter, the deer come down
for food; hungry for love,
they stalk the traffic on perfect legs,
doe-eyed, nowhere near
appropriately scared.

I slow my Villager on Knight's Hill,
a buck taps his white cane
off the centre divide;
I cannot hear you over all the noise
in both our lives.

You once said to let Nature
take her course, and I know
that water finds its own level,
but this — I grip the steering wheel
with both hands, the buck reaches

high ground, I breathe a sigh,
then a next breath, and a next,
into the absence,
into the rising tide,
and rather than wait

for sadness to cover my eyes
from behind, I drive on
toward the village of the world
where enough food, a warm bed,
put me in with the lucky few.

All day the deer play
catch-me-if-you-can on the Miracle Mile;
Spring rain shakes out the trees,
and I can almost touch the veils
that ripple down between our lives.

Coming home, old sun
lays her gold leaf on every stone,
unpins her hair into the wind;
any morning now, the first faun
folded quietly by the road like a stillbirth.

Before the Wind

Under the flimsy
layer of noise I wear
I charge the depth of silence.

Outside Goldfield
the first Joshua trees
stand guard over nothing.

Snow rushes at our lights;
the tumbleweeds crouch and dance,
we turn, drive from the known,

down Lost Section Road,
swimming into our withdrawals,
Leopardi's fathomless quiet.

The sky flares yellow,
losing light over Wild Rose Peak;
moths hover at the mystery white flower.

My ship is turning,
big and blind in the night,
so monstrous it blocks out sound.

By Walker Lake, the first water,
we enter the final silence;
bittersweet to sail on it.

Searchlight

Death Valley, 1997

In the shadow of the Panamints,
hushed at a thousand feet,
this is the garden where we'll walk
as though nothing broke, no beads spilled.

Salt rings on the Devil's Golf Course,
we pick our way along the delicate path,
the desert lands evenly on the skin;
I snatch up my flame, I put it out in the cold.

Fingers burning as we unravel ourselves,
set all our carrying down;
we weighted ourselves so heavily,
and then we dived in.

Send a searchlight across the alluvial plain,
the swept area shivers;
I find myself on the valley floor,
hunched on the salt pan, breathing again.

Get me to a child's place, a schoolroom, a well of safety,
here among the toys and alphabets I can say
in pain like darkness
I have nothing to draw on today.

Flying low and soundless over our history,
the bareness, the bare bones, the shabby deeds.
Hushed, still as a blade, I read the cracked truth:
we are undone, no one can bind us.

Patagonia

I drive by the reservoir, the hills
smudge into an early dark,
frog song springs out of the loaded air
and the rain begins,
long skinny filaments on my windowpane.
What surprises me now
is how I can forget the course is changed:
I think we are still heading
for the Cape of Good Hope, banderole aloft,
on our mettle, tacking into the game.
Instead, we ride anchor off Fire Land,
Patagonia, with its dry squall lines,
its sheep, Magellan's desperate straits,
its Indians in their overshoes — this is the place
all Winter breaks out.

Dillon Beach

The high September tides
carved themselves another beach,
this one strewn with green weed; the wind
drove old ghosts down the throat of the bay;
over against Point Reyes the sailors choked on the rocks.
I thought I'd shatter.

Near Chimney Rock the lightman trimmed his wick
by a Frenchman's lens,
but I was missing; I was not in our house.
I left. Nobody expected that.

Lying in a friend's high room
I knew in the sunlit chambers there is ease,
with every seventh wave comes balm.
I reached for the light,
loosened the ropes of the past
and let it drift, bumping the sides of the night.

Down on Dillon Beach
I mounted my search.
I picked up shells but they were frail,
fragments, and I wanted something whole;
I chose stones but they were cold.

Wood is warm and was once alive. I liked that.
I found myself a half-moon,
silver-grey, sickle-grained driftwood clavicle.
It sat inside my closed palm
and hid between my shoulder blades;
it took my pain,
rolled it around in the edge of the waves
and wore it smooth in the shallows.

Last Winter

Last Winter in my cottage, all that trouble;
hearing rain, the swallowing dreams,
I saw no more than my single life, lived in a line.
I loved, with and without reserve,
a man who set fires. After I turned,
he went where he always went,
back into the burning building.

The Signing

The wet December grass is underfoot,
a plane writes a straight line across the single blue.
On the Sky Trail
each leaf shivers in the shade;
there is too much news.

The shadows arch and stiffen toward noon,
a great weight hangs by a skinny thread.
When it swings
laughter will be banished from the afternoon
and the quiet will be layered with dread.

Spell out the many words for the end of love,
scrawl them on the white sheets furling from the rooves
of those who cry:
'Hold back the pen that writes your union off
along the dotted line; there is another way!'

Snow begins, tiny dry grains,
catching in the creases, massing in a drift,
a weight of evidence against us,
and my signed name
is all I have to say.

Harmless

Tired, I am
tired. You've been hearing that for years,
my way of saying: Enough, I shut down.

Today I drew air,
swore before the law we could not be saved.
A stranger asked
if each would hold the other harmless.
Should I be angrier?

I've stopped at a simple place,
the rinsed fields, the boats hung to dry.
Out of a threadbare fog
I come into light of my own,
I lie on my back, unharmed,
tinkering with the shades of it.

Then home, some digging in the dark
garden, a moth on the window frame,
all that intricacy on its way to dust.
The dog sighs as though
she knew it would end thus,

and from the house a measure of Couperin
shakes out fragments of a lost day.
What else is missing — Beethoven, Beethoven, Bach —
I open the dusty piano to play
the fugue, both hands holding
memory's commands, my hand, my other hand,
they are letting you slowly go,
they are holding you harmless,
and what they play here
is a piece of nothing.

Dragonflies

Coming into the meadow from the dark wood
I smell the fires, they're eating the tall ash
grove; the dense magnolia blooms
are wreathed in the heat of their own perfume.
I can stand their flaming.

Up from the long grass come
dragonflies, I see through their wings;
maybe my life was damaged when I took it out
of the box, an odd arc that cannot be described,
the tightness of being cut loose.
I doubt. I do not want to be untied.

Beyond the fires I see the pall of rain,
a bird skeets in the willows.
It's not that I'm trapped by the promise of pain —
I can ride that out, across the interior,
my angel placing his hands like that
on either side, listening to the ordeal —

but after so much conflagration,
burning my head, and my eyes, and behind my eyes,
lights in the different corners, all that sensation,
I recognize that mine is the hall of the insane;
roaming at night I pass my lit window.
I'm there on the bed. I know I'm watching.

Was all this written in the chemical code,
the mind a feeble image of the artist's
great and subtle plan? I turn in my cell,
the rain has drunk the bitter fires down,
I turn again. Up from the cold ground
come dragonflies.

Seven White Deer

It's like a death.
It has that finality,
that lost limb ache.

I'm standing now,
stripped as a telephone pole,
wires low, live from my cranium
through my bones, their marrow,
to my soles. But I'm cold,
there's ice on the way down.

Over the dark yellow, nearly mid-March horizon
the sun laid a burnished path
into the West all yesterday.
You wrote to me: On the Meadow Trail
seven white deer — and I was the only one
you knew who would care.

I'm carrying poppies, criminal yellow,
and loose-skinned sweet little Jamaican fruit.
The starriness of Spring leaves,
my store of unusual words, these treasures
keep my birds singing, strung like obsidian,
high on the wires along the levee road
where the river mourns in the reeds.

I made you a wooden heart,
oak, stout as your own,
then it was time to start
tearing our promises down.

Choose us an empty room
in the house where we were born,
over the hammering pain
I will whisper of our undoing,

and wish this were the burial day
of all our sensitivity,
our belief, our desires,
our consuming fears,
and our brief, eternal five years.

Alstroemeria

I put myself back in time, firmly in October,
at a house with its own strand;
apricot sky, blue cold, gentle water,
a shell in my hand, pearl's mother.
I am always leaving Ireland.

Time moves at its old speed
but the journey home takes longer.
I wear the ring you gave me,
the gold and platinum band
you promised against all harm.

Today is better than yesterday,
November, the eleventh slate.
In my house it seems impossible to break
I am composed
of such durable material,

and I wear Peruvian lilies,
brash, slowly opening,
yellow with a darkening red,
they bend down lower, new leaves
turn over, butterflies fan out.

The River Daughter

Slow burn, low ebb
days like today
when rain is general
and the giddy edge in range,
my heart is chained.
I lock it down
when dusk swallows shadows across the town.

Days like today,
I try to recall how you were a piper man,
out there in the dazzling afternoon,
everyone followed. I shut my door repeatedly
and, in the mornings, there you were,
laughing, spilling daylight, deep inside my room.

Now, in my second life,
I cannot dance for a week with a brittle man.
My river is dammed,
behind my wall
dark waters rise over a drowned world.

Here in the centre you spun out of laughter,
I cannot rekindle our blue flame.
My fragile craft shudders, memories threaten
to pull me under on days like today,
so I rein the river in,
breathe out, and go on longing,
deep in the room of the river daughter.

Limpets

Barcelona, October 1997

Whatever I put in these empty rooms
they are still these empty rooms.

Old sun deep on the neighbour's porch,
recessed sun in the Spanish palms.

One, two little girls, a boy
stood in their baby shoes in the sand,

sang themselves the glittering sea,
hid pink shells in their sandy pails.

There I saw their father's smile,
limpet hands at the ice-cream stall.

Long pale nights in my brother's house,
toys on the verandah, chairs all round.

I washed my hands of the milky past,
shiver and ripple of lies dissolved.

I took a leap at the heart of it,
woke myself from years of sleep.

Giddy with choice in the morning light,
I got right down to truth and belief,

took things out of the empty rooms,
let in the sunlit afternoons.

Hawkesbury River, NSW

I was a schooner,
I was a rigged cutter with sixteen oars,
fire on a bed of earth in my hold.

I liked to be on the river without purpose,
the swell from the mailboat washed at my hopes;
I ran my oars idly through the mangrove swamps.
At Milson Island the kids from town
fished from the jetty with silver spools,
white prawns for bait,
and all news carried equal weight.

On the Bauer Point foreshore I berthed in the dawn,
the river revealed at its own pace
its purpose; beyond the mouth,
the trades laughed in the face
of the great winds that govern hurricane and calm
and fanned into motion my knot of flame.

I was moved by the tide beyond fear,
left my old ways by the shore and struck out
with a good tailwind, plain sailing
for the Solomons and their bold promises —
whale teeth, coconuts, and pearls.

Big Island Dance

1

I live at the top of the town.
When the fire goddess blows her wrathful horn
I stay down,
I sit on my beautiful hands.

I may be alone
but every night
I see the planet's last exotic drunken light
and I dance to my own ragtime.

2

When we came
crickets pulsed in the o'hia trees,
among the koa in the warm breeze
we were young, tasting the muskmelon.

We climbed Kilauea
dipping our hands in the wet breath,
promising love unto death,
crossing our hearts.

3

From my lanai
I watched myself as your ghostly wife
dressed in plumeria's fragrant white
dive in the bowl of fire,

and when I rose,
veiled in the flicker of tikki lights,
I was shorn and clean, free
of your promised heart.

    4

I live at the top of the town,
dine on the fruit that falls;
when the mountain roars
I drop my gaze.

I may be alone
but every night
I see the last of the unending light
and I two-step into the dark.

Approaching Thirty

On a journey to another country,
deep into the untouched orchards,
having exhausted sleep
I crouched in a chair till dawn,
the world as a house around me,
memory held impermanent.

It was not shown to me
how to move on, how to leap;
mid-air I was given the secret
words in their order.

But in time you have to go further,
meet fire as a rival, maybe a salamander,
not flinch at the small reminders,
gravel thrown by the handful:
age is irrecoverable,
I will never be wiser.

Almost thirty,
swimming in the deep pool
of my wife tears, honest and ordinary,
I found in the many chambers of myself
with the fears connected to nothing
forty thousand reasons to go on living.
I felt them collect, just out of my field of vision,
and wait for me there, dark blue, dark green.

PART THREE

234a Railroad

Emergence

It was there all along, great peace.
I wear it again, I turn around in it.

What changes inside when the spark lights,
the fizz of a match coming up,
candles growing their yellow robes.

Curled up cottonball alone and warm,
at sea, rowing sporadically,
it feels like shipwreck and being found,
it feels like round rings falling into round.

On Limantour beach
I pay to be hidden with dollars of sand,
birds fly the razor breaks of the waves.
I can find what I placed in the dark,
I can dive by the light of Venus.

I like where I am sitting now,
but at your door I got shy,
left after knocking lightly.
One day you might hold me

in your piano hands,
life all arpeggios and resolving chords.

Venus Awake

after Delvaux's 'Venus Asleep' (1944)

Everyone's in a spell but I'm not caught.
Make the hammers yield your deep summer music
across the creek, I in my kitchen, listening
and listening; I have never listened before.

It could have been anything,
dulcimer, cithara, musical stones,
but the past decided that it was piano I owned,
the yellowing ivories that brought you to my home.

I was unprepared,
tired, almost beyond forgiving.
In my high-ceilinged room
you brought everything into tune;
now the notes fall where they should fall,
a weightless and effortless flow.

I know how late it is
to dream of little death and desire.
Up on my wall
Venus and the skeleton and the dressmaker's girl
inhabit the moonlight of Delvaux's unreal
tableau. You can come to my door
any pale silver night,
you can enter there without call.

Musketeer

On the dance floor, against the mirrored wall,
a sharp intake of breath, you are
the breaking of it all, the dawning;
I close my eyes, the darkness is forgiving,
then we start dancing.

Black velvet musketeer, lace at the wrists,
rearing up on a dark horse,
a knight by your promises,
always wheeling unshod in from the cold
with my single rose.

I want this mantle around me,
here in the space I stepped to warily.
Later you said my hunger made you, my desire,
we slept on the maple floor
in a shaft of sunlight, a couple of shadows wide.

Halfway through my life in these deep waters,
uncharted, pitching in this generous storm,
singled out for more delight than I can fathom,
immeasurably calm, I see my definite course
by your lightning, vivid and forked and sheeting.

234a Railroad

I have always wanted this, always belonged here,
the crookedness, the rough tile floor.
The nightlight shines up yellow through the weeping fig,
lays cat shadows on the blond wood,
picks out the scattered notes to myself,
charitable and remissory. In this sanctuary
I'll heal, I know I'll heal.

Mine is an art that leaves itself behind,
my bones in their narrow home,
my snatch of spirit in its ossuary.
I'll watch this brightwork turn and turn
always new facets to the falling sun,
and though mere words can weigh life's colours down
I'll think of mine as I reached for them,
and caught them sometimes, and let them go.

One year in this lucky house,
birthday to birthday, all May mornings
up Suncatcher Ridge to the windmill farm,
sometimes an hour at the brimming drawers of the past
full of the spells of wet stone, big trees down,
bottles and footfalls and blood orange tears;
when I look back honestly
the present settles clear in me.

Today Spring cheered on Railroad Avenue,
I climbed the foggy dawn,
then home for coffee
in front of the bathers who hung in the Stein salon
(Matisse said Cézanne was the best of them all)
and with a red trowel
I buried my last shred of doubt in the warm ground.

Architrave

This is a story of weight
borne by a load-bearing wall.

The connection is not
of water or air

or even our tightly interwoven
histories of love and fear,

but of stone on stone.
I take your hand,

but in truth I have the measure
of your every bone

and no load is too great,
for balance has become our home,

and I can say without complaint:
bear down on me without doubt

for I hold your hand up to the light.
See how our bones fit together?

How We Meet

That first day in the hills above Forest Knolls
we were burnt onto the yellow grass,
our silhouettes two kites in the vast blue surprise,
hearts in an updraft,
white hopes fluttering behind.

Yes, I said, I was married,
dressed in snapdragon innocence.
I dreamed, and that was me
sleepwalking, needing to be
slapped awake.

So, you said, making music
in the labyrinth of my inner ear,
there are innumerable possibilities here;
and on the bay shore of my peninsula
you strung six pearly beaches —
Chicken Ranch, Teacher's,
Shell, Shallow, Pebble, Heart's Desire.

When the days grew smoky and shorter
we met in a blue café.
If this happiness doesn't last,
you said, expect a deeper goodness.

In a Mexican mountain town
we lay in the still whirlpool of a whitewashed room,
the scarf of our siesta working loose.
Meet me at Santa Domingo, you said,
down by the church,
in the angelic peach and apricot of earliest sunset.
I knew of no better waiting.

If ever we meet in a glass house
with stones for hands
or crossed talk
I'd like it heard that I know how it feels
to be charmed, I'd like our love
to let us leave that place unharmed.

What I Move To

On the Sydney Harbour front,
getting used to water,
I'm trying to learn the summer's colours
in the dirty light between the rocks,
but they escape me.

It is curious,
balancing on another hemisphere
between familiar abyss and abyss,
some days, minimal clues, then the dawning —
you're a rhythm on the other side
that I am moving to.

In the Botanical Gardens
plants known only from man's handling,
cultivation, intervention.
The site of my life is alluvial soil:
forest red gum and swamp mahogany grow,
sun filters through the high fan palms —
and they said that nothing would thrive there.

Being in the Cave before Time

I caught a glimmer of you on the wet walls
lit with a triple wick, wax going up in smoke,
and I sketched you with the burnt end of my stick.

This was before time,
before your name, or mine,
our dwelling, the bed of stone.
It was all I knew at the start,
the blunt stick and charcoal likeness in the rock.

I was in a primitive place, grey with some yellow,
loving the honest light of day
and the bluer light that came so late,
streaming in the yawn of the cave,
old moon, stepping on stones,
folding your long form on the glistening slate.

One night the moon tripped.
I stood in the teeming space with sharpened breath,
dark and medicine, medicine and dark,
reaching out with my eager hands
I brushed against you on your stone,
you caught a hand, all thumbs, and traced the scars,
you sighed because it was warm,
you'd thought me cold, so still in my waiting,

and I let your touch cool my weather veins,
and I let you press a greenstone in my palm,
turning over the amulet of calm
as the moon slid out her reddened eclipsed eye.
I could have lived like that in the dark.

Eight Months, Fifteen Days

Since we cast off in this fragile craft
to practise the delicate art
of rowing, you have had
at your command my fair seamanship,
my three-part harmonies.

The moon is full;
around the moon a moving blue circle
spirographs a thousand other moons;
you and I are counting.

The shores we left
are where scrubland meets the lake,
the ground is soft and ashy,
between the grasses, delicate
birdsteps, wild dog tracks;
Indians fish at the edge for cutthroat trout.
They know we can't own the land,
we just walk there.

Your hand stirs. Time is slow here.
We hesitate to go ashore.
The moon is emptying.
You ask for my name again,
with my free hand I unbutton it
in a moment, I lay it down.
You say, 'Look! Look at Orion!
There's his club, his belt, see his two feet?'
I can't follow, I think I'm going
somewhere I never told myself about.

Back on dry land
sulphur water springs from the rock,
hot and slick to the touch.

We walk apart,
our different rhythms keep us alight,
our common spirit leads us to the tallest rock,
we have spilled our lives from the top
and watch them fall.

A Thousand Letters

I dreamed you into my cell,
smelling of rain,
silvering the key in your palm,
beckoning.

The guards in their paper houses
lowered me in here and I hit the stone
end of the well; ocean of hurt,
too much for one room.

What would I do with an ordinary day?
Out on the streets,
remembered blue of the dawn,
all roads lead to the sea.

A night's wind has softened the sand
but I leave no tracks, my thumbs are bare
of prints, my photograph dissolved,
my bones erased.

The freedom is too thin, the dream frail,
the shadows escort me back:
but there, at the end of fiction,
dawns an impenetrable light,

a letter from you, a thousand letters,
truth rises unobstructed,
bountiful and benevolent,
it winds white lilies around me.

Nereid

When I died I put on sandals
too delicate to be worn,
for my safe passage over,
for my coming up at dawn
arm in arm
with Helios from the rounded water.

My organs were sealed
in the canopic jars, my airy heart
weighed in the balance against Maat.
How to compare her truth, her good,
against my humble art.

I was seventeen crossing the waterways
into the field of reeds.
I passed Osiris, murdered by Seth,
he lay on a lion, rescued by Isis,
who crowned him King over death.

Then the bronze bands of living got narrower.
I turned on my left side,
my eyes in line with the painted eyes
on the tamarisk wood, ivory
under my head, rolled scrolls between my thighs,
begging for sanctuary.

I wondered would it be flight that would lift me
up and over the beautiful world,
thermals that would hold me there,
but it was love took me, kept me airborne,
love and loss, and it was violent trust
that let me pass.

Still Life, Yellow Quilt

School's out; tables with their chairs on top,
blackboards black, playgrounds spinning ghosts,
the hot wind blows a dust-devil up,
the air's a sonnet.

Out at Chimney Point the water's beryl blue,
our house is drawn against the tides with pencil strokes,
our summer daughters stream into the sea,
down in the tide pools, fishing for stars,
our son's a roamer.

Somewhere between owl-light and lark,
before the first sounds of an August dawn,
Death comes in and sits down
and when she takes my hand she's warm.

I know I should be lying with the ones I love
on our yellow quilt in the seaside house,
temporary in sleep, unapproachable,
with the white waves washing music to our doors
and the gulls keening;

but I am drawn in spite of my concern
to welcome in my home this temperate guest
who counsels me to lay my burdens down
for it is not my time;

and it's not because my life is a script
that she has written out, line by line,
and laid upon the page for me to read,
but because I know I can't hold onto it
as I swim upriver to the place where I was caught;

and the weight of my life bears suddenly down
and its lightness bubbles up; my guest is gone
with the dawn broken loose from the night sky
on another languid, apricot August day.

So I lie down on the yellow quilt, my arms
loosely about their heads in the simple room;
Raphael should have painted us, golden and true,
with the white waves washing easily back and forth,
and the gulls crying.